Text by Lois Rock
The story of the Nativity can be found in the Bible in
Luke's Gospel, chapters 1 & 2, and Matthew's Gospel, chapters 1 & 2
Illustrations copyright © 2005 Carolyn Cox
This edition copyright © 2005 Lion Hudson

The moral rights of the author and illustrator
have been asserted

A Lion Children's Book
an imprint of
Lion Hudson plc
Mayfield House, 256 Banbury Road,
Oxford OX2 7DH, England
www.lionhudson.com
ISBN 0 7459 4850 2

First edition 2005
10 9 8 7 6 5 4 3 2 1 0

A catalogue record for this book is available
from the British Library

Typeset in 13/18 Baskerville MT Schoolbook
Printed and bound in Singapore

My Book of
Christmas

Written and compiled by Lois Rock
Illustrated by Carolyn Cox

LION
CHILDREN'S

Contents

Mary of Nazareth

The little town of Nazareth stands on a hilltop not many miles from Lake Galilee. In the springtime, the fields around it are bright with wild flowers, and sheep nibble the green grass. By summer, the fields of barley have ripened from green to gold. Soon, grapes hang from their vines as clusters of purple. Finally, the olives are beaten down from their grey-green trees and pressed for oil. Winter comes. After the summer heat, everyone is glad to have cool and rain.

This was the landscape that Mary knew, some 2000 years ago. She lived in one of the flat-roofed houses in the town with her family. They were respectable people and, from the time Mary was born, they began to think about one very important question – whom should she marry?

It was their job to find out which families had a suitable son. They wanted to find a husband who would take good care of Mary when she was grown up.

At last, when Mary was still a girl, they came to an agreement with the carpenter's family. Their son Joseph would marry Mary when she was the right age.

The two watched each other growing up. Each week they saw each other across the synagogue. This was the place where everyone went to worship God. They listened to people reading aloud from the scriptures. In this way, they learned of promises that God had made to the people long ago:

The Lord who made you says this:

    'Do not be afraid: I will save you. You are my people and I know each one of you by name. Troubles will come, but they will not defeat you. Times will be hard, but you will not be hurt.'

Mary wanted to believe that was true. She was dreaming of a happy life ahead: it was not long to the time when she would be a wife and, after that, a mother...

Her own mother was not so sure how easy her life would be.

'We are a defeated nation,' she explained wearily. 'Look at the Roman soldiers you see everywhere. They obey orders from the emperor in Rome who rules our land. He rules all the world, as far as I know. We have to pay to keep him in luxury and his army well fed. Your Joseph will have to work to earn enough to look after you and pay taxes to Rome.'

Mary still went on hoping that all would be well. After all, it was God who had promised to take care of them all. 'Remember that bit in the book of the prophet Isaiah,' she reminded her mother, 'the promise that God will one day send a king to rescue our people – you know… the one that goes like this:

The people of the shadowlands
are walking in the light.
For you have brought them joy, O Lord,
and led them out of night.

Now celebration fills their days –
a harvest feast all year.
Their enemies have fled away,
and love replaces fear.

A child has now been born to us!
A boy to be our king!
The prince of peace for evermore,
his praises we will sing.

'Perhaps I will live to see God's king come and change the world,' Mary said to her mother.

'Perhaps,' said the older woman. She didn't sound at all sure. Then she smiled. 'Perhaps your cousin Elizabeth will be the mother of the king. After all, it's a miracle that she's pregnant at all… everyone thought she was too old ever to have a baby.'

It was something to dream about.

About Advent

Advent is a word that means 'coming'. It is the name some Christians give to the four weeks before Christmas. Advent is a time to look forward to remembering Jesus coming to this world as a baby.

During Advent, Christians remember that Jesus' own people, the Jews, were looking forward to the coming of a king. For hundreds of years, stronger nations had beaten them in war. They longed to have a king like David of long ago. He had beaten all their enemies.

In fact, wise and holy men called prophets had told them over and over again that God would send a king. Their word for God's chosen king was 'Messiah'. By the time of Mary and Jesus, many people in the world they knew spoke Greek. The Greek word for Messiah was 'Christ'.

During Advent, promises of a king from the

books of the prophets are read aloud in many churches.

One Advent tradition is the Advent ring. It consists of four candles arranged around a central candle. One candle is lit on each of the four Sundays before Christmas. The central candle is a symbol of Jesus and is lit on Christmas Day.

Advent Prayers

Advent prayers are about trust in the many ways
God helps people and rescues them from all kinds
of trouble.

> Come, thou long-expected Jesus,
> Born to set thy people free,
> From our fears and sins release us,
> Let us find our rest in thee.
>
> *Charles Wesley (1707-88)*

Dear God,
When the night is dark,
remind me of bright daytime.
When the winter is cold,
remind me of warm summer.

When troubles are all around me,
remind me of your blessings,
then bring me safely
to a place of love and peace.

God's love reaches high to the heavens,
God's faithfulness touches the sky,
God's strength keeps me safe
from the things that I fear
till the danger and storm have passed by.

Based on Psalm 57:1, 10–11

When I lie down
I sleep in peace
for God is by my side
to keep me safe
from every harm
and always
be my guide.

Based on Psalm 3:5

Christmas in the Bible: Luke's Story

The Christmas story of Jesus' birth is found in two books of the Bible. The two stories are often retold as one. Christians sometimes call this the Nativity story – the word 'nativity' simply means 'birth'. They begin with the story told in the book of Luke.

Luke became a Christian after Jesus' lifetime on earth, when Jesus' closest friends, the disciples, began spreading the news about him. Luke wanted to help spread the news as well and decided to write a complete account of Jesus' life. To do this, it seems that he used a book that had already been written. This book is in Bibles today – the book of Mark. However, Mark's book says nothing about Jesus' birth.

So Luke used other ways to find out about

Jesus. He spoke to some of Jesus' disciples, and some people think he also asked Mary for information.

Luke tells about an angel coming to give Mary the news that she will have a son, about the journey to Bethlehem, about Jesus being born in a stable, about the shepherds on the hillside and the message the angels told them. Luke also tells of the baby Jesus being taken to the Temple, where two people recognized that he was the promised Messiah, the Christ.

The following stories are retold using information from Luke.

(You can find out about the other book – the book of Matthew – on page 60.)

A Visit from an Angel

'Only three months to go till your cousin has her baby.' Mary's mother seemed to talk of nothing else. Except the possibility of her becoming a grandmother, of course.

'Now, when the time comes for you to have a baby…'

'I'm not even married yet,' Mary reminded her. 'You've got some waiting to do.'

'I'm just thinking about names. You see, your cousin Elizabeth is going around saying that her baby is definitely a boy. Her husband is Zechariah, so if it is a boy – and we'll know in three months' time – he should be called Zechariah too. Now, when you have a baby boy…'

'If, mother, if.'

'… you could call him Joseph. But now I've been thinking, Joseph's family is descended from that of King David…'

'Hundreds of years ago.'

'… so in fact it would be quite acceptable to pick a name that shows the link between your baby and King David.'

Mary decided to go and find some jobs to do on her own. She needed a bit of quiet.

Suddenly, an angel appeared.

'Peace be with you,' said the angel. 'God is with you, and God has blessed you.'

Mary edged away, trembling with fear. Who was this strange visitor? What did these words mean?

The angel spoke again. 'Don't be afraid, Mary. God has chosen you to be the mother of a very special child. You will have a son, and you will call him Jesus. God will make him a great king, like King David of long ago. His kingdom will never end.'

Mary was thinking as fast as she could. She knew what the angel was saying... that God had chosen her to be the mother of the king who would rescue all her people. At the same time, she knew that wasn't true.

'That can't happen,' she protested. 'I'm not yet married –'

'God will make all this happen,' explained the angel. 'For that reason, your child will be known as the Son of God. Remember that God has blessed your cousin Elizabeth, and she is going to be a mother at long last.'

'I will do as God wants,' Mary agreed. Then the angel went away.

Soon after, Mary found out that she was pregnant. She decided to go and visit her cousin Elizabeth.

'Hello!' she called out, from the open doorway.

Suddenly, Elizabeth felt her own baby move inside her. More than that, it seemed to Elizabeth as if God and all of heaven's angels were in the house with her. She came hurrying out to find Mary, calling as she ran.

'God has blessed you,' she exclaimed, 'and God will bless the child you are going to have. My own baby is jumping for joy inside me.'

Then Mary knew for sure that all the angel had said must be true.

She sang for happiness.

Mary's Song

My heart praises God, and my soul is glad:
for God has remembered me;
and from now on everyone will say that I am blessed.
God has done great things for me;
God will do great things for us:
for God is on the side of those who are poor;
God helps those who have no one else to defend them.
God will bless our people, as promised so long ago.
God will bless us all.

Dear God,
Help me to understand what you want me to
do with my life, so that I, like Mary, can help
bring your blessings into the world.

Teach me to help the poor.
Teach me to protect those who have no one to
defend them.
Amen

Angels

The Bible says that angels are heavenly beings. God created them even before making the world we know. Several Bible stories include angels who bring people messages from God. Sometimes they appear just like human beings, and people don't recognize them as angels at first. Other times they seem to shine brightly, and people are overawed by them.

The angel who comes to visit Mary is one of the angels in the Bible who have a name: Gabriel. Many people think that Gabriel was also the angel who visited the shepherds, but Luke's story does not say so.

In Matthew's story of Jesus' birth angels speak to people in dreams – to Joseph and also to the wise men.

In the Bible, Jesus says that every child has
an angel looking after them – a guardian angel.
Here are two prayers that mention guardian
angels.

Angel of God, my guardian dear
To whom God's love commits me here,
Ever this day be at my side
To light and guard, to rule and guide. Amen

Traditional

Lord, keep us safe this night,
Secure from all our fears;
May angels guard us while we sleep,
Till morning light appears.

John Leland (1754–1841)

The Name 'Jesus'

The angel told Mary she should name her baby 'Jesus'.

In fact, 'Jesus' is simply another way of saying the name Joshua, and has always been a popular name. It means 'God saves'.

For Mary and the Jewish people, the name was a reminder of a great hero of days gone by: Joshua was the people's leader after Moses; he led them into the land of Canaan, where they made their home.

He is famous for his victory at the battle of Jericho. On that occasion, so the story goes, God told the people to march silently round the city every day for six days, the white-robed priests leading the way. On the seventh, they did the same, but ended with a great shout. By a miracle, the city walls fell down and the people were able to win the battle. As a result, the name was also

a reminder that everything people hope for depends
on God's saving them, not their own strength.

Mary – and Jesus – would probably have
pronounced the name as you would say
'Yehoshua'.

The Journey to Bethlehem

Mary's return to Nazareth sent her mother into a frenzy of worry.

'It's as if everything's gone wrong at the same time,' she said, wiping away a tear. 'I let you go to visit your cousin, thinking that will be helpful to her while she's expecting, and when you come back everyone can see that you're expecting too.'

'I told you what I saw and heard,' said Mary, trying to stay calm. 'This baby will be a blessing to us all.'

'Now there's this new order from the Roman emperor about a census. We've all got to put our names on his list. It's a tax list, isn't it, so this time next year we'll all be worse off.'

'Joseph says he can always get work,' said Mary. 'Hmmm.'

Mary knew that no one had any reason to be angry with Joseph. 'He's keeping the promise to marry me,' she said cheerfully, 'even though he's not the baby's father.'

But her mother would not be comforted. 'So because you're *going* to get married, the law says you must go and put your names on the tax list in his family's home town. So I lose you while you travel to Bethlehem. Who knows when you'll be back.' She gave a deep sigh.

'Well, let's get everything ready for your journey,' she said. 'You'll need to have some baby things ready. Now where did I put them?'

It was a long journey to Bethlehem.

'I think it will take us six days,' said Joseph.

'Maybe five,' suggested Mary. 'After all, we don't know exactly when the baby will come,' but I'd rather be *in* Bethlehem than *nearly in* Bethlehem.'

So they travelled as far as they could each day. But Mary felt more and more tired. It seemed that everyone else was going faster than they were.

When at last they reached Bethlehem, Joseph set about finding a place to stay. 'I'm sorry,' said one person. 'I've already got as many people staying with me as I've got room for.'

'It's a pity you didn't get here sooner,' said another. 'I've taken as many guests as possible. But I know someone else who has rooms to spare.'

'Please help us,' said Joseph to the third person. 'You can see that Mary is expecting a baby any day. We must find shelter somewhere.'

But there was no room for them. In fact, there was no proper room anywhere in Bethlehem. In the end, the only place that anyone could offer was a room that was normally kept for the farm animals.

Mary sank down wearily into the straw. 'At least it's indoors,' she said gratefully.

In that poor and humble room, Mary gave birth to her son. She wrapped him in strips of cloth, to swaddle him snugly.

'Where can I put my baby to sleep safely?' she asked.

Joseph found a manger which still had some hay in it for the animals to eat. He swept it clean and lined it with straw.

And so Mary used the rough stone manger as Jesus' first cradle.

Christmas Carols

For hundreds of years, Christians have celebrated the birth of Jesus by singing carols. Here are two:

Away in a manger, no crib for a bed,
The little Lord Jesus laid down his sweet head.
The stars in the bright sky looked down where
    he lay,
The little Lord Jesus asleep on the hay.

The cattle are lowing, the baby awakes,
But little Lord Jesus, no crying he makes.
I love thee, Lord Jesus! Look down from the sky,
And stay by my side until morning is nigh.

Be near me, Lord Jesus, I ask thee to stay
Close by me for ever, and love me, I pray.
Bless all the dear children in thy tender care,
And fit us for heaven to live with thee there.

Traditional

Silent night, holy night,
All is calm, all is bright
Round yon virgin mother and child;
Holy infant so tender and mild,
Sleep in heavenly peace,
Sleep in heavenly peace.

Joseph Mohr (1792–1848)
Translation from German: Anonymous

The Christmas Crib

Nowadays, it is very usual to see a crib scene: it may be a display of little model figures showing Mary, Joseph and Jesus, and all the visitors who come to see the baby.

Many people think that the first person to create a living picture of the Christmas crib was a man called Francis. He lived about 800 years ago in Assisi in Italy. He lived the life of a beggar monk, travelling from place to place telling people about Jesus and encouraging people to follow Jesus' example of love and kindness.

One Christmas, he asked a wealthy man to lend him a barn, and asked people to come and play the part of the people in the Christmas scene. The people who came saw a heavenly light shining from the manger – as if, once again, heaven had come to earth.

The Shepherds on the Hillside

Out on the hillside near Bethlehem, some shepherds huddled against the wall of the sheepfold. They pulled their cloaks closely around them to keep out the cold night air.

'There's talk in the next valley of a lion that's been taking sheep,' said one.

'Pah,' replied another. 'I've been a shepherd for thirty years. I've never seen a lion between Bethlehem and Jerusalem. It's jackals that are the problem. Jackals and sometimes wolves.'

'And thieves, of course,' said the third. 'There's so many people taking part in the emperor's census, you don't know who's around these days.'

They all murmured in agreement and went back to watching silently.

The stars shone brightly in the sky. A wisp of cloud blew across the moon. 'Nice and peaceful tonight,' said one. He closed his eyes, hoping to doze for a moment.

Out of nowhere, a light shone – a light of brightest gold. The men gasped and gripped their staffs. There was someone there, bathed in a halo of shining light.

'Say who you are,' ordered one shepherd, angry with terror. 'Or I'll fight you!'

The figure in the light smiled gently. 'Don't be afraid,' it said. 'I am here to bring you good news. Today, in Bethlehem, God's promised king was born – the Christ, the rescuer. You can go and see him… a baby, wrapped in swaddling clothes and lying in a manger.'

Suddenly, other figures appeared in the light.

Angels! Angels from heaven itself. Their voices rang out, like sweetest music in the night air. 'Glory to God!' they sang. 'Peace on earth.'

It was as if time had stopped. It was as if heaven had come to earth. It was as if the shepherds were looking right into the shining loveliness of God.

Then everything vanished, and the night was grey and shadowy again. The moon sailed out from behind a wispy cloud. The shepherds looked at one another.

'Did you see that?'

'Did you?'

'Do you think it's true, what they said?'

The only way to be sure was to go and find out. They tied the gate to the sheepfold shut and pulled a pile of thorny twigs in front of it. Then they headed up the hill to Bethlehem.

Few lamps were burning at that time of night. The shepherds peered into every lighted window... and then they saw him.

There was a baby, lying in a manger. There was a man there, gazing into his face. He looked up when he heard a noise and saw the shepherds.

'Come and see,' he whispered, opening the door. 'My name is Joseph. This is Mary, and our new baby boy.'

The shepherds tiptoed nearer. 'You'll never

believe what brought us here,' the shepherds began to explain. But the more they told, the more the woman's eyes shone as if she not only believed every word but understood it too. Perhaps it was true. Perhaps this baby was the promised king.

As the shepherds strode back out to where their flocks were, they broke into a song – a hymn they knew, a hymn of praise to God. Now the ancient promises to their people were all about to come true.

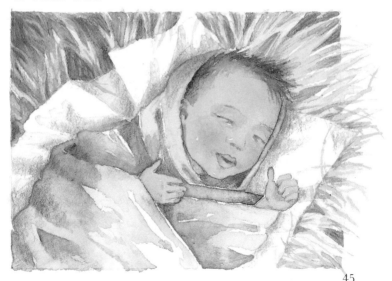

Go with the Shepherds!

An azure sky,
All star bestrewn,
A lowly crib,
A hushèd room.
An open door,
A hill afar,
Where little lambs
And shepherds are.
To such a world,
On such a night,
Came Jesus –
Little Lord of Light.

Mary I. Osborn

Let us travel to Christmas
By the light of a star.
Let us go to the hillside
Right where the shepherds are.
Let us see shining angels
Singing from heaven above.
Let us see Mary cradling
God's holy child with love.

Christmas Day

The festival people call
Christmas remembers the
time that Jesus was born.
One tradition is that he was
born at midnight – the moment
when Christmas Eve ends and
Christmas Day begins. For this

reason many churches have services that begin
a little before midnight so they can celebrate the
very hour.

Christmas Day is celebrated in many countries
on 25 December. In fact, the Bible does not say
what time of year Jesus was born. The first
followers of Jesus did not have a special festival
celebrating his birth: Christmas celebrations only
began hundreds of years later.

It is likely that Christians decided to have this
happy festival at the time of their old pagan

midwinter celebrations. At the darkest time of the year, it seemed a good idea to celebrate the birth of someone who, they said, was the Light of the World.

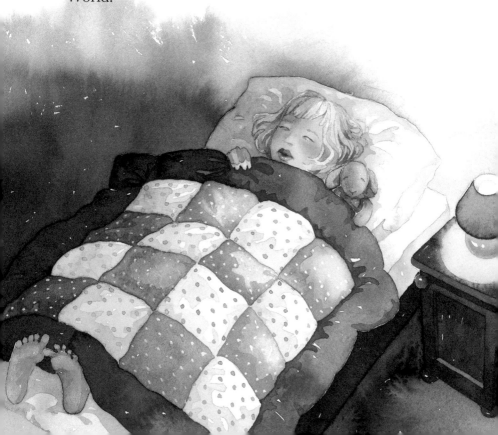

Christmas Animals

Several animals are linked to Christmas.

The only ones that are actually mentioned in the Bible stories of Jesus' birth are the shepherds' sheep – and, in the Bible story, the sheep stay out on the hillside. However, many pictures of the Christmas scene show the shepherds bringing at least one or two sheep with them!

Because Jesus was born in an animal room, it seems likely that there were farm animals there too. The tradition is that there was an ox and an ass, because one of the prophets of Jesus' people had long ago said that the ox and the ass would recognize their true master. Often, Mary and Joseph are shown travelling to Bethlehem with an ass.

In pictures of the first Christmas you will also often see doves in the rafters of the stable. There are two reasons for this. One is that a dove is a symbol of the Holy Spirit. When Jesus was grown up he was baptized, and the Bible says that God's Holy Spirit came down upon him like a dove. The other is that a dove is a symbol of God's promise to bring new life: it was a dove that brought the first green leaf back to Noah after the flood.

The wise men are often shown making their journey to Bethlehem on camels. It is true that people from lands to the east frequently travelled through the desert on camels, but the Bible does not say if the wise men did.

Christmas for the Birds

For people, Christmas is a time of feasting.
Outside, when it is winter, it can be a hungry
time for the birds. Many people make Christmas
the time to begin putting out extra food and
water for them. In return, the birds gather at the
feeding places and sing their songs as merrily as
any carol!

God bless the birds of winter
that hop across the snow
and peck the fallen seeds and fruits
of summer long ago.

God bless the birds of Christmas:
when all the trees are bare
they gather in our gardens
and their carols fill the air.

Baby Jesus in the Temple

Mary's baby was one week old. It was time for the naming ceremony. There was no question about what to call him: Jesus, just as the angel had said.

Not long after, it was time for another ceremony. Long ago, God had given the people many laws. One of them said that every firstborn son had to be dedicated to God. Mary and Joseph took the baby Jesus to the Temple in Jerusalem as the law required.

The very same day, an old man named Simeon decided to go to the Temple.

'I feel in my heart that God wants me to go today,' he explained. Simeon was a good man, and he believed that all the promises God had made the people would one day come true. So

of course he was expecting God to send a king to
rescue them all. He was also quite sure he would
live to see that king.

Simeon was in the Temple when Mary and Joseph arrived, carrying the baby Jesus. As soon as he saw them, he knew that Jesus was the one.

'Please let me hold the baby for a moment,' he said to them. He looked down at the face of the infant Jesus with love and respect. He said a prayer: 'Thank you, Lord God, thank you. Now I know that I can die in peace. For now I have seen the one whom you have sent to save us, the one who will bring your blessing to all the world.'

'What do you think he means?' whispered Joseph.

Mary shrugged slightly. 'I'm not sure; but it all seems to fit with what the angel said to me,' she replied.

Simeon looked up from gazing at the baby. 'This child has been chosen to speak the truth from God,' he explained. 'Not everyone will welcome what he has to say. His birth has brought us joy, but in the end there will be bitter sorrow as well.'

He gave Jesus back to Mary to hold. She clasped her baby tightly. He was so precious to her, she would do anything to protect him. But she knew the stories of her people. She remembered some of the stories about prophets. They had spoken words of truth from God, but people hadn't always wanted to listen. All too often the prophets had been mocked, ignored and even rejected. Was the same kind of thing going to happen to Jesus?

Her wondering was interrupted. An elderly woman had begun calling out to the crowd. 'God be praised,' she was saying. 'There is the child who will save us! There is the one who will set us free!'

All around, people were beginning to murmur. Old Anna was known to be both good and wise. Could her words be true?

'Whatever Jesus has been born to do won't happen just yet,' Joseph comforted Mary. 'We shall go home to Nazareth, and there he will grow up along with other children. He will go to school to learn to read, and I will teach him to be a carpenter.'

And so it was. Jesus grew to be strong and wise, just as any mother would want.

Christmas in the Bible: Matthew's Story

There are two stories of Jesus' birth in the Bible, and one of them is in the book of Matthew.

No one really knows who wrote this book. Like Luke, who also wrote of Jesus' birth, the writer of the book of Matthew borrowed a lot of information from the book of Mark – but that begins when Jesus is grown up, so the writer of Matthew must have got his story of Jesus' birth from somewhere else.

One thing is clear: the writer of Matthew wanted to show his readers that Jesus was truly the promised Messiah. Everything that the prophets of old had said about the Messiah comes true in Jesus.

The following stories are retold from the information given in the book of Matthew.

Joseph's Story

Joseph was meant to be working. He was meant to be laying the wooden rafters in a large new house. The owner wanted it finished soon, and he was impatient at how long the builders had taken.

But Joseph couldn't keep his mind on the job. He kept thinking about how all his plans had been ruined. One day, everything seemed happy and straightforward. He was going to marry Mary, and then they would have a family. He would work hard and they would have enough to live comfortably and everything would be fine.

Then the bad news had come. Mary was pregnant. It certainly wasn't his baby she was expecting. She didn't seem to have any explanation that made sense.

He sighed heavily. 'I could let everyone know what has happened, and then no one will make me marry her, because she's clearly broken her promise to be faithful to me.' That would be easy enough.

It would be easy for him, anyway. But not easy for Mary. That was the problem. She would be in public disgrace. Everyone would gossip about her.

He thought again. 'I could just break off the engagement quietly,' he decided. 'Her own family will still have to sort out what happens to her next, but maybe they will find some relatives who are willing to let her join their household. That way she will have a chance to build her life again.'

That seemed like the best idea. Feeling more confident, Joseph got back to the building and worked as hard as he could to keep his mind off his sadness.

Joseph was glad to see the darkness creep across the sky. Time to go home. Time to sleep. Time to forget all the trouble of the daytime.

But even in his dreams he kept thinking of Mary, of the happy life that might have been, with a strong young son running to greet him at the end of the working day.

Then, in his dream, he saw a stranger standing next to him. 'Joseph,' said the stranger. 'You don't need to worry. You can marry Mary. It is because of God that she is pregnant. Her child is God's own Son. You are to name him Jesus.'

God's own Son, thought Joseph to himself. God living among us.

Then he remembered something he had heard in the book of the prophet Isaiah. A young woman would become pregnant, and her son would be known as 'God with us'.

All at once, he knew that the stranger was an angel and the message was true. He felt happy again – happier, in fact, than he had ever felt before. The very next day he went straight to Mary's house to explain that he still wanted to marry her. He promised to be a good husband, and always to take care of Mary and her child.

About Joseph

Matthew (and Luke) both list the ancestors of Joseph. Although the lists are not exactly the same, they both say that Joseph's family roots went back to the great King David. He had been a great soldier and had put an end to the wars with his people's enemies.

But none of the books about Jesus says much about Joseph. People believe that he was a carpenter because Mark's book says that Jesus was a carpenter, and usually boys did the same job as their father.

People also believe that Joseph was still alive and married to Mary when Jesus was 12 and he travelled with his parents to Jerusalem for a special festival. (In fact, Joseph is not named in that story.) However, none of the books about Jesus mention Mary having a husband by the time Jesus is grown up. When Jesus is on the cross, he even asks one of his disciples to take care of her as if she were his mother – something that makes people think she was a widow by then.

Because of all this, it is traditional to think of Joseph as being much older than Mary. However, the usual age for boys to be married was between 14 and 16, so he may have been a teenager when Jesus was born.

Searching for a King

Joseph's home town was Bethlehem, the place where David had been born. It was also the place where Mary's child, Jesus, was born.

Not long after, some travellers arrived in the nearby city of Jerusalem. They had a puzzling request. 'We are looking for the baby boy who is going to be king of the Jews. Can you tell us where he is, please?'

No one could help them. 'We haven't heard of a baby king!' they replied. 'The only king around here is Herod; and even he has to take orders from the emperor in Rome.'

The travellers would not be put off. 'We're sure a king has been born. We saw a star rise in the east, and it is quite clear to us that it is a sign of a newborn king. He is to be a king like no other, and we have come to worship him.'

The Travellers

Matthew's book does not give many clues about the travellers who came looking for Jesus: only that they studied the stars and came from lands to the east.

As a result, there is a tradition that they were magician scholars from the lands of the old Persian empire – in the area that is now Iran and Iraq. For this reason they are sometimes called the Magi.

Another tradition is that they were kings, but there is nothing to prove that this is true. Yet another is that their names were Balthazar, Melchior and Caspar, and that one of them had dark skin. Again, there is nothing to prove this.

There isn't even any proof that there were three of them! This tradition comes from the fact that they gave three gifts to Jesus.

However, everyone agrees that Matthew shows

them to be non-Jews who clearly saw that Jesus
was a king who must be worshipped.

On to Bethlehem

Everyone was gossiping about the travellers and their quest, and very soon King Herod heard the news. At once he grew angry. He did not want any rivals. He was prepared to get rid of anyone who threatened his power. He had done so before, and he was ready to do so again.

But first he must find this so-called king. He called together the priests and religious teachers.

'Tell me more about the promises made by the prophets, the ones about God sending a king, a Messiah. What clues do they give us? Do they say where the king will be born?'

'They do indeed,' the men replied eagerly. 'The prophet Micah names the very place. Bethlehem.' And they unrolled one of their scrolls and read aloud.

'Bethlehem…' Herod tapped his fingers. The place was close enough, but how would he know which baby was meant to be the king? Who could recognize him? Herod thought long and hard, then snapped his fingers towards the guard.

'Fetch me those travellers. I need to use them. But I don't want anyone to know that they've been talking to me. Bring them to the palace without anyone seeing.'

In the dead of night, the travellers were brought to the palace. Herod asked them many questions: what was the star, when did it first appear, could they see it now, what *exactly* did it mean. He listened to every little detail they had to tell him. Any information could be vital.

'Now,' he said, 'I have something useful to tell you. The child is to be born in Bethlehem: that is what one of the great prophets of old predicted. But if the news leaks out that the child has been born, every mother in Bethlehem will claim that it's her son. You and I need to act together. You go to the town and find out which is the real king. Then I can go and worship him.'

Herod smiled at his cunning plan.

The travellers set out on their way at once. It was still night, dark and shadowy. Then, to their great delight, the clouds parted and a bright star shone out.

'There it is,' they cried. 'It's shining on the road to Bethlehem. Everything is pointing us in the right direction!'

The star led them to Bethlehem, and then hung low over one little house. The sun was just beginning to show on the skyline as they called out at the entrance. 'We're looking for a baby boy,' they said. 'We believe he is here.'

Joseph was a little startled. He came to greet them. 'Well, my wife has a young child,' he explained. He smiled. 'He's a lovely boy. Do you want to see him. He's awake and with his mother.'

When the travellers saw Jesus, they knew they had found the king they were looking for.

'This child is born to do great things,' they said. 'We have gifts to offer him.' They presented gifts of gold and frankincense and myrrh.

As everyone gazed at the little boy Jesus, morning sunlight came flooding into the house.

Gold, Frankincense and Myrrh

Many people think that the gifts given to Jesus have a special meaning.

Gold means power and riches. It was meant to show that Jesus was going to be a king.

Frankincense consists of little blocks of amber-coloured tree resin. When it burns, it gives off sweet-smelling smoke. Priests burnt frankincense as part of the ceremonies at the Temple to worship God. It was meant to show that Jesus was going to be a priest, helping build a friendship between people and God.

Myrrh looks like a pink powder. It is made from the sweet smelling gum of the myrrh plant. Myrrh was used in perfume and incense and also

to prepare bodies for burial. It was meant to show
that Jesus was going to be important not only for
his life but also for his death.

What Can I Give Jesus?

Lord Jesus,
The wise men brought you gold:
Let us use our riches to do good.

The wise men brought you frankincense:
Let our prayers rise like smoke to heaven.

The wise men brought you myrrh:
Let us seek to comfort those who are sad
    and grieving.

Lord Jesus,
You have given us so many rich gifts:
Let us use them to do your work in this world.

The wise men read the skies above,
and now we read their story
of how they found the prince of peace,
newborn from heaven's glory.

We come, as if to Bethlehem,
to offer gifts of love
to make this world at Christmas time
a piece of heaven above.

What can I give him,
Poor as I am?
If I were a shepherd
I would bring a lamb;
If I were a wise man
I would do my part;
Yet what I can I give him,
Give my heart.

Christina Rossetti (1830–94)

Epiphany

There is a tradition that the arrival of the wise
men is celebrated twelve days after Christmas.
The festival is called Epiphany. The name comes
from a Greek word that means 'showing', because
it remembers the time Jesus was first shown to
non-Jews – a sign that he had come as a king to
everyone in the world. In fact, the arrival of the
wise men is often included in the main Christmas
story told around Christmas Day.

Some people think that Christmas decorations
should be taken down in time for Epiphany.

Escaping from Herod

The travellers who had followed the star could not have been happier. They had found the little king they were looking for. Joseph and Mary had welcomed them as special guests.

'Such a difference between the way we have been treated here in Bethlehem and in Jerusalem,' said one. 'I always had the feeling we were being spied on when we were in the big city.'

'We probably were being spied on,' said another. 'People here have been telling me about Herod. He has secret guards everywhere. There are terrible tales of his cruelty. He thinks nothing of killing anyone who gets in the way of his ambitions.'

'I'm not looking forward to seeing him again,' said a third. 'We'll have to begin the journey home tomorrow.'

They spent the day getting ready and enjoyed one last night sleeping in comfortable beds.

The following morning, they began loading their belongings. One of them called the others to sit down with him. 'I have something important to tell you,' he said. 'Something that makes me want to change our plans.'

The others listened, curious to find out what he had to say.

'I had a dream last night, and in my dream I had a warning not to go back to Herod. I woke up feeling fearful. If we go and tell him our news, something awful will happen.'

One of his companions frowned. 'We did give our word,' he argued.

Another shook his head. 'When I gave my word, I believed that Herod wanted to welcome the new king as much as we did. Now I am not at all sure.'

'I am afraid for our own safety,' said the first, 'but even more afraid for Jesus.'

The mother came to say goodbye carrying her little son. When they saw his smiling face they knew what they must do.

They took a different road out of Bethlehem and returned to their own country without visiting Herod.

Joseph had walked a little way with the travellers. They were glad of his help in finding the right road.

'Are you sure you don't want to go back to Jerusalem?' he asked. 'The new Temple there is a wonderful sight.'

'We've seen Jerusalem,' they replied.

'What is more,' added one, and here he leaned down towards Joseph, 'we don't trust Herod. And, in my opinion, neither should you.'

The words had made Joseph worried. Everyone knew that Herod was ruthless. What might Herod do that would bother him and his little family?

That night, in a dream, an angel spoke to Joseph: 'Herod will be looking for the child, Jesus. He has heard that there is a newborn king. He will want to kill him. You must take Mary and Jesus far away. Go to Egypt. Stay there until I tell you it is safe to leave.'

At once, Joseph got up. He woke the family, hurriedly packed their few belongings, and took the road that led south to Egypt.

It was the right thing to do. Herod soon realized the travellers had tricked him. He was afraid that somewhere in Bethlehem a mother was raising a child to be a king: a threat to him.

In a terrible rage, he sent his soldiers to go to Bethlehem and kill all the baby boys under two years old. That way, he would be safe: safe from everything; safe for ever. So he imagined.

A few years later, Herod died. In a dream, an angel told Joseph it was safe to return. 'We will go to sleepy little Nazareth, in the hills of Galilee,' he explained to Mary and Jesus. 'That will be a good place for us to live.'

Joy to the World

Joy to the world!
The Lord has come;
Let earth receive her King.
Let every heart prepare him room
And heaven and nature sing,
And heaven and nature sing,
And heaven, and heaven and nature sing.

Isaac Watts (1674–1748)

Goodbye Christmas

God, our loving Father, help us remember the birth of Jesus, that we may share in the song of the angels, the gladness of the shepherds and the wisdom of the wise men.

Close the door of hate and open the door of love all over the world.

Let kindness come with every gift and good desires with every greeting.

Deliver us from evil by the blessing which Christ brings and teach us to be merry with clean hearts.

May the Christmas morning make us happy to be your children and the Christmas evening bring us to our beds with grateful thoughts, forgiving and forgiven, for Jesus' sake. Amen

Robert Louis Stevenson (1850–94)

A Bright New Year

The stars that shine at Christmas
Shine on throughout the year;
Jesus, born so long ago,
Still gathers with us here.
We listen to his stories,
We learn to say his prayer,
We follow in his footsteps
And learn to love and share.

Noël is leaving us,
Sad 'tis to tell,
But he will come again,
Goodbye, Noël.

The kings ride away
In the snow and the rain,
After twelve months
We shall see
them again.

Traditional French